Original title:
Island of Eternal Summer

Copyright © 2025 Creative Arts Management OÜ
All rights reserved.

Author: Nathaniel Blackwood
ISBN HARDBACK: 978-1-80581-479-5
ISBN PAPERBACK: 978-1-80581-006-3
ISBN EBOOK: 978-1-80581-479-5

Shores that Hold Forever's Touch

On sandy banks where laughter sings,
The seagulls dance with silly springs.
A flip-flop toss, a kite on high,
Mismatched socks wave 'hello' to the sky.

With sunburned noses and goofy hats,
We barter tales with grinning cats.
The ice cream melts, we lick the cone,
While giggles echo through the stone.

Where Time Sways to a Gentle Rhythm

Time's a friend, it twirls and bends,
With waves that laugh and never end.
A clock's tick-tock? It's a joke, you see,
As crabs dance sideways in glee.

The sun sets slow, a lazy swirl,
While mermaids flirt with a golden pearl.
We sip on smoothies, flavors gleam,
In this quirky, sun-soaked dream.

The Realm of Unfading Days

In a land where shadows play peek-a-boo,
And flowers wear hats of every hue.
The clouds are marshmallows, soft and bright,
As we chase the horizon, pure delight.

Giggles float like bubbles in air,
Life's a ride on a merry-go-share.
With a wink and a nod, we sway this way,
In the realm of sunshine's endless ballet.

Cocktails of Color in the Air

Drinks with umbrellas, oh what a sight,
Topped with cherries, everything's right.
Riding cycles with wobbly flair,
As rainbows twirl in the salty air.

A parrot squawks jokes with flair and grin,
While turtles throw confetti for wins.
The laughter spills into the sea,
Where fun is the key, for you and me.

Echoes of a Boundless Breeze

Seagulls squawk with such flair,
They steal my snacks without care.
Sandcastles wobble, then they drop,
Mermaids giggle, "You just can't stop!"

Sunburned noses in a line,
Ice cream dribbles, oh, so fine.
Flip-flops flop, socks on the shore,
Who needs shoes? I want to soar!

The Utopia of Infinite Light

Cocktails mixed with silly straws,
Dancing dolphins give applause.
The tide rolls in, the tide rolls out,
With beach balls bouncing all about.

Palm trees sway, they seem to dance,
In this place, we laugh and prance.
With every wave, a ticklish tease,
Oh, how I wish to ride the breeze!

A Garden Where Seasons Forget

Sun hats perched atop my head,
I grow tomatoes in my bed.
The flowers giggle, colors bright,
Bees wear sunglasses, what a sight!

Butterflies playing hide and seek,
All week long, not a peak.
In this patch where time stands still,
We juggle joy; it's quite a thrill!

The Peace of Perennial Play

Kites are flying (or they're stuck),
Kids all laughing, what a luck!
The sunbeam's glow on silly pranks,
Tickling toes, giving thanks.

Shells in buckets, treasures found,
Ghost crabs dancing all around.
With every splash, a heartfelt cheer,
Endless giggles, summer's here!

A Daydream in Brilliant Warmth

Basking on the sand so bright,
A seagull steals my snack outright.
With a laugh, I toss my hat,
Who knew a bird could be so fat?

Sunburnt toes and ice cream drips,
Hula lessons lead to funny slips.
Under sun, I take a roll,
In this heat, I lose control!

The Lore of Bright Horizons

Tales of pirates, tales of gold,
But my drink's got ice and it won't be cold.
A coconut tree sways in glee,
It might just be plotting against me.

Flip-flops squeak with every stride,
Riding waves is quite a ride.
If I wipe out, I'll surely pout,
But then I'll laugh, I'll laugh it out!

Radiance Within Reach

The sun is bright, my drink's a shell,
Caught a wave but fell so swell.
A crab scuttles, teasing too,
Chasing me as if it knew!

Sandcastles rise and then they flop,
A sun hat flies, where did it drop?
Mysteries of beach life untold,
In this heat, I feel so bold!

Tidal Muses of Sublime Heat

Ocean's whispers, they call my name,
But the sunscreen blurs my claim to fame.
I try to pose, look oh-so-cool,
But trip and fall, oh what a fool!

The horizon dances, a beautiful tease,
While I search for chips with ease.
Laughter echoes with every wave,
In this chaos, I feel quite brave!

Full Moons in the Heat of Joy

The moon hangs low, a big yellow bulb,
Like a giant's cookie, a sweet, silly grumble.
Crabs dance in circles, all wearing their shades,
While dolphins play leapfrog, in splashy parades.

With laughter so loud, you might lose your hat,
A parrot squawks jokes, and that's just the cat!
Sandy toes wiggle in a rhythmic delight,
As fireflies twinkle like stars in the night.

Trails of Sunshine Through the Palm Fronds

A sunbeam slips by, as a squirrel makes leaps,
Chasing shadows with gusto, while the whole world sleeps.
The ocean waves giggle, tickling the shore,
As flip-flops declare war on the sand once more.

Bikinis on turtles play peekaboo fun,
While waves whistle tunes that make dolphins run.
Coconuts roll like bowling balls in the breeze,
And even the crabs join in giddy tease.

Calm Waters of Unchanging Skies

The pond is a mirror, reflecting the pranks,
Where frogs wear top hats and give out their thanks.
A turtle in shades sips a drink with a grin,
While fish throw a party—a synchronized swim.

The clouds are like marshmallows, fluffy and bright,
As seagulls tell jokes in their feathery flight.
A hammock swings gently, inviting a snooze,
Right next to a crab that just can't stop the blues.

An Oasis of Laughter and Love

In a coconut grove where the giggles abound,
A sloth tells a story, though he moves all around.
The breeze whispers secrets with a ticklish flair,
While monkeys throw coconuts, giving a scare.

A parade of bright colors leads to the sea,
Where fish wear their bowties and dance with glee.
Laughter erupts as they twirl and they spin,
With joy in their hearts, let the silly times begin!

Dance of the Immortal Sun

The sun wears shades of vibrant gold,
As it dances and twirls, quite bold.
With flip-flops flapping, it rules the day,
Spreading laughter in a silly way.

Coconuts giggle, and palm trees sway,
While crabs try to join the bizarre ballet.
Even the seaweed gets caught in the cheer,
Tickling toes, spreading joy far and near.

Starlit Evenings on Endless Shores

Stars whisper secrets, a cosmic embrace,
As they twinkle and waltz in this magical space.
The waves come in with a soft, playful shout,
As sandcastles giggle, and tourists pout.

A starfish dreams of being a star,
While fish make jokes from afar.
Shells come together for an evening of fun,
Sharing tales of mischief beneath the sun.

Embrace of Tropical Whispers

The breeze tells tales of a clumsy parrot,
Who chews on a flip-flop like it's nectar of carrot.
Hammocks sway gently in laughter and glee,
As the sun sets low with a cup of sweet tea.

Bananas do yoga with the mangoes around,
In this place where absurd holds the crown.
The laughter of fruits fills the lush green scene,
And beach balls bounce like they're living the dream.

Melodies of an Unfading Twilight

Twilight sings with a saxophone shell,
As the moonlight dances, casting a spell.
Turtles rock out on the sandy dance floor,
Doing the shuffle as they ask for more.

The horizon blushes at the grand show,
While jellyfish jiggle, stealing the glow.
With a wink from the stars, the fun won't stop,
In this goofy paradise, forever on top.

Dreams Cradled in Sunbeams

A seagull's scream, a sunburned face,
Chasing crabs in a sandy race.
Flip-flops flapping, laughter flies,
Coconut drinks and silly sighs.

Pineapple hats and swimming flings,
Tanning lines like rainbow rings.
Sunscreen battles, good times swell,
In this warm, wacky carousel.

Canvas of an Unending Day

The clock melts like a scoop of ice,
Time here just isn't that precise.
A nap means napping at midday,
While ants throw a parade, hooray!

Flip the canvas, paint the sky,
With shades of laughter as we fly.
Mismatched socks and sunhat dreams,
Dancing wildly in sunbeams.

Vegetation Bathed in Golden Light

The palm trees wiggle, sway and jig,
One wears sunglasses, oh so big.
A monkey swings to steal a snack,
While flowers giggle, that's a fact!

Bees buzz on a nectar spree,
Flirting with flowers, oh, so free.
Green leaves whisper hilarious tales,
Of how to sail with wind-filled gales.

Twilight Unfolds in Paradisiacal Glow

As twilight dances, shadows prance,
Even the stars laugh in their chance.
A hammock sways, a labrador snores,
While sandcastles trade in their wars.

The moon, a radiant pizza slice,
Calls out to crickets with advice.
Rats in tuxedos hold a soirée,
As the night sings, 'Let's dance and play!'

Where Time Surrenders

Sunbathers dance with a floppy hat,
While crabs steal snacks, imagine that!
A seagull swoops for a chip or two,
And the beach ball waves, 'Hello to you!'

Tanned folks nap on their beachy thrones,
Counting sheep or perhaps sea phones,
A beach towel fortress, built with flair,
In search of mermaids, we will dare!

Sandy toes and laughter's golden glow,
As sunburns paint faces in rows,
A game of catch with a splashy twist,
Tides giggle softly, can't resist!

Time takes a break; the sun's on parade,
Belly flops and swims, the joyful charade,
We may forget where our shoes have flown,
But this laughter-filled shore, we'll call our own.

A Canvas of Timeless Wonder

Brushes made from seaweed and dreams,
Splash colors that burst like bubbling streams,
Palm trees sway to a calypso beat,
As crabs take the dance floor with their tiny feet.

Funny sights at an oceanic fair,
Where flamingos wear hats, beyond compare,
A sandy Picasso with flip-flop feet,
Creating art even fish think is neat.

Seashells grin under the sun's warm gaze,
As kids trade jokes in a sunshine haze,
The laughter echoes, rich as the sea,
'This is our masterpiece!' shouts the crab with glee.

The sunset hums a tune of delight,
With hues of purple and pink so bright,
Each sip of coconut, sweet and divine,
While jellyfish waltz, 'This beach is mine!'

Notes from an Everlasting Dusk

Evening falls like a soft giggle,
As fireflies start their twinkling wiggle,
Sandy feet shuffle towards the light,
While shadows play games of peek-a-boo night.

Toasters roar with the scent of s'mores,
As laughter spills from open doors,
The stars above wear their shiny best,
While the moon checks its list, simply jest.

Balloons float high in the chilled sea breeze,
Tickling the noses of giggling bees,
A hammock swings, strung with tight knots,
'The perfect spot for our silly thoughts!'

As dreams dip into the horizon's embrace,
We'll dance with stars, no need for a grace,
With every chuckle, we plant a new seed,
In this whimsical dusk, we are freed!

Taste of Salted Air

Seagulls squawk, stealing fries,
Beach umbrellas wave goodbyes.
Sandy toes and sunburned backs,
Who needs shoes? We've got snack attacks!

Waves crash in their silly dance,
Dolphins giggle in their prance.
Sipping drinks with goofy straws,
Laughing loudly, just because!

Surfboards tumble, surfboards crash,
Wipeouts make a thunderous splash.
With a load of giggles on the side,
We ride the waves, no need to hide!

The salty air, a scent so sweet,
Creamy sunscreen slathered on feet.
Under the sun, we all declare,
Life is best with salty air!

Echoes of Joyful Laughter

A flip-flop lost in the sand,
Who knew it would take such a stand?
Kids scream, running from the tide,
Dodging waves, what a wild ride!

Laughter echoes, pops like fizz,
Caught a crab? Now that's the biz!
Sandcastles built, then toppled down,
With giggles loud, we wear our crowns.

Ice cream drips on sunny days,
Sticky fingers in a daze.
Chasing seagulls, yelling 'mine!'
Salted fun, oh, how divine!

As sun sets low, we do our dance,
In flip-flops, it is our chance.
Echoes of joy ring in the air,
This laughter here, beyond compare!

The Light That Knows No End

Sunshine beams, a burst of cheer,
Beach balls fly, have no fear!
Sunkissed hair, a tangled affair,
In this glow, we simply stare.

Picnic snacks all spread around,
Seagulls hope for crumbs they found.
With silly hats and shades so bright,
We soak in laughter, pure delight!

Fruits on skewers make us grin,
Watermelons tossed like win.
Pranks unfold beneath the sun,
Who knew that fun had just begun?

With the sun that never quits,
We dance and wiggle, making fits.
The light that knows no end is here,
Wraps us tight in summer cheer!

A Haven of Blossoming Heat

Hats that wobble like a drift,
In heat that gives our cheeks a lift.
Tropical drinks with tiny umbrellas,
We toast to life, like silly fella!

Palm trees dance to a breezy tune,
Blossoming laughter under the moon.
Sunburns happen, what a plight,
Yet all we do feels so right!

Tanning lotion, a slippery game,
Someone shouts, "You're looking lame!"
We giggle as we rub it in,
Sunshine teasing, a timeless win!

In this haven where smiles grow,
Bikini-clad in the sun's warm glow.
We bask in fun, bloom, and heat,
Forever chasing laughter sweet!

Perpetual Sunshine's Embrace

Everyday's like a beach day,
Except the sand's made of cake.
We surf on waves of lemonade,
And pancakes gleefully shake.

Sunscreen smells like bubblegum,
While seagulls wear tiny hats.
The crabs compose a funny drum,
And dance with bright yellow spats.

The Sanctuary of Never-Ending Warmth

Flip-flops chirp a silly song,
As we waddle down the pier.
The sun just smiles all day long,
Cheerful rays, nothing to fear.

Palm trees gossip in the breeze,
About how tan they all are.
Coconuts mock our allergies,
While sipping on fruit jar.

Whispers of a Coral Paradise

Fish wear sunglasses in the sea,
And teach us how to glide.
The corals giggle with such glee,
As turtles already slide.

Underwater karaoke nights,
Where jellyfish rock the stage.
They sing of bubble-filled delights,
And glow with every age.

Days Unfurling in Vibrant Hues

Colors burst like popping snacks,
As the sun paints skies in joy.
Beetles ride on surfboard backs,
And laughter flows like a toy.

Mango trees throw parties bright,
As friends gather all around.
This whimsical, cheerful sight,
Leaves no room for grumpy frown.

Secrets Beneath Coastal Skies

Beneath the waves, a crab does dance,
With clumsy moves that make us glance,
A fish in shades of pink and blue,
Winks at me, says, 'What's wrong with you?'

The seagulls squawk a silly song,
As if to say, 'You don't belong!'
I wave my arms, they mock my stance,
And fly away, a daring prance.

Turtles chat about their plans,
To host a ball in water lands,
They wear top hats made of seaweed,
While sea stars laugh, it's quite the deed!

Under the sun, we find delight,
With jellyfish floating, quite a sight,
Each bubble pops with laughter bright,
Secrets shared in coastal light.

The Art of Wind and Water

The wind decided it would play,
To tickle waves and make them sway,
A surfboard riding on a breeze,
Is just a fish in rushing freeze!

Watercolors splash on the shore,
With each wave crash, a joke to explore,
A dolphin flips and suddenly trips,
In a belly flop, it surely zips!

Seashells giggle, buried in sand,
As crabs conspire, they form a band,
They tap dance on the ocean's edge,
While barnacles sit, a ruffled pledge.

The art of fun, it's clear to see,
In every wave and every plea,
Nature laughs in ways so true,
With wind and water, dreams anew.

Festivities of Forever Light

Under the sun, there's quite the scene,
With pineapples wearing crowns of green,
A party starts as coconuts grin,
And lemurs swing, it's time to begin!

Tiki torches dance in the breeze,
As crickets play their symphony tease,
With monkeys serving drinks in shells,
They spill the juice and ring the bells!

Each wave retreats, then rushes back,
In pink and gold, they leave their track,
And dolphins bring a cake of foam,
Saying, "Happy day! You're never alone!"

Festivities last from dawn till dusk,
With laughter ringing, hearts all husk,
Life is a journey, let's take flight,
In this realm of forever light.

Unbroken Circles of Laughter

Rounding the shore, we gather round,
With giggles echoed, what a sound!
The sandcastles stand, proud and tall,
Then come the waves, and they all fall!

A crab plays tag with a clumsy dog,
Both slipping and tumbling through the fog,
The sun sets low, the colors blend,
As laughter rings, it seems to transcend.

Seagulls swoop low, with treats to steal,
As kids run fast, it's a big deal,
In circles unbroken, we all take part,
The joy of simple things warms the heart.

In laughter's embrace, we find our bliss,
Returning to shores, we reminisce,
With stories that swirl like the tide,
Together forever, we take the ride.

The Sea's Embrace

The waves laugh loud, a cheerful jest,
Seagulls steal fries, what a bold request!
Shells wear sunglasses, sipping their drink,
The fish are gossiping—oh, what do you think?

Sunbathers flip like pancakes on sand,
They yell at crabs who don't understand.
With sunscreen battles, we fight for a glow,
But here's the trick: it's a slippery show!

Frolicking dolphins throw back their heads,
Doing backflips while we lounge in our beds.
One hops on a board, thinks he can surf,
But lands right beside me—what a splashing turf!

As sunsets paint the sky with orange hues,
We dance on the shore, in flip-flop shoes.
With voices that echo, we sing round the fire,
And the ocean laughs back—sure, we're all wired!

Footprints on Forever Beaches

Each morning I wake, with thoughts of the shore,
But my breakfast is sand—just a bit too much more!
My footprints are silly; they jiggle and hop,
Like they're chasing crabs that just want to stop.

Building a castle with moats and tall flags,
But the tide shows up, carrying bags.
"Excuse me," I shout, "That's my home for the day!"
It chuckles and swirls, washing dreams away.

Sunscreen battles with bottle cap foes,
Slipping and sliding, oh, who really knows?
The sand between toes, a tickling tease,
I run from the seagulls, "Hey, that's my cheese!"

The horizon winks, as the ice cream truck nears,
While laughter erupts, igniting our cheers.
With footprints in circles, we dance in delight,
Forever on beaches, where shadows feel light!

Sunlit Dreams of Paradise

Under a sky where the sun likes to play,
I tripped on a beach ball—it didn't obey!
My sunhat flew off, a quick flying saucer,
Landing on a bystander—a frequent confuser!

We sip on coconuts, with straws on the side,
While mermaids yell, "Hey! Please join us to ride!"
But I'm feeling too lazy, my towel's my throne,
With no ambition to swim, I'll just stick to my cone.

The BBQ sputters, hot dogs take flight,
Some seagull must think he's a marvelous sight.
He swoops with a purpose, but it's all a surprise,
When he dives for our snacks and then leaves with no prize!

As the sun burrows down, the day's slipping fast,
We stumble our way to the sky's vibrant cast.
With dreams full of giggles and sand in our hair,
We'll cherish this madness, a fun-loving affair!

In the Arms of Perpetual Sunshine

Towels unfurl like sails in the breeze,
While I'm stuck in laughter, struggling to sneeze.
The coconut drummers start tapping away,
And the beach bums take bets on who will be gay!

A crab on my foot, his grip is so tight,
I shout like a champion—what a silly sight!
He pinches my toe, as if to declare,
"Claiming this spot, now you can't go anywhere!"

The pineapple drinks have umbrellas so bright,
While I'm still choosing the best one to bite.
A competition brews for the tallest sand tower,
Who knew it would tumble with just one stray shower?

As the day fades softly and stars play their tune,
We gather 'round fires, cooling selves like a boon.
With giggles and stories, dreams take their flight,
In this sun-drenched haven, everything's just right!

Sunlit Shores of Endless Bliss

On beaches where the flip-flops dance,
And seagulls plot a silly prance,
We sip our drinks with tiny straws,
While sunlight plays its shining cause.

Old palm trees whisper cheeky jokes,
As sunburned tourists laugh at folks,
Who thought the tide would hold them in,
But now they wade with grins and fins.

The sandcastles built with much pride,
Tumble down like dreams that slide,
As kids declare their royal crown,
While parents feast on ice cream brown.

So join the dance beneath the sky,
Where every laugh is a well-earned high,
In crazy hats and shades so bright,
We toast to joy from morn till night.

Timeless Tides of Laughter

The waves come in with giggles loud,
As surfers try to impress the crowd,
But end up tangled in their boards,
With goofy grins and silly hoards.

A crab in shades struts on the sand,
While sunbathers offer a helping hand,
To those who've misplaced their sunscreen,
And now resemble a lobster scene.

The beach volleyball bounces around,
Where missed hits create laughter profound,
And every serve is a wild surprise,
As players dive with wide-open eyes.

With beach towels that flutter and flop,
We gather near the ice cream shop,
For flavors that make our taste buds sing,
In this crazy, fun-loving fling.

The Haven of Endless Dawn

In a place where mornings giggle and stretch,
With coffee cup jokes that never fetch,
We rise and shine with a silly yawn,
While the sun winks at the sleepy dawn.

The roosters crow in disco style,
As tropical birds add to the smile,
While yoga mats become slip-and-slide,
And downward dogs just can't abide.

Juice stands serve up jokes with zest,
While folks debate on who's the best,
At tossing fruit in a blender fast,
Creating drinks that leave us aghast.

We laugh as time meanders slow,
In this haven where giggles flow,
With every sunrise bright and clear,
We embrace each moment, full of cheer.

Reflections on a Sea of Gold

The ocean shimmers with golden hues,
As fishermen tell the silliest news,
Of mermaids spotted with bubble hair,
And treasure chests that vanish in air.

Sunset picnics bring food fights galore,
As sandwiches soar and chips hit the floor,
With laughter echoing into the night,
While stars join in, twinkling bright.

Our shadows dance on this sandy stage,
As crabs throw parties, full of outrage,
While we forget what the world is like,
And play charades with a friendly spike.

With every wave that crashes ashore,
And every giggle that we adore,
We find ourselves lost in this bliss,
In a sea of laughter, we can't resist.

Calm Waters and Endless Sunshine

The seagulls gather, squawking loud,
They think they're stars in a feathered crowd.
Sandcastles tumble, what a funny sight,
As waves roll in, they giggle with delight.

Beneath the sun, a beach ball flies,
It hits the ice cream, oh what a surprise!
Melting drips down, a sticky mess,
We laugh and swim, in pure happiness.

Lemons are dancing, they roll on by,
Pair them with sunshine, give it a try!
With jokes about tans and flip-flop woes,
The ocean chuckles, as the good times flow.

So grab a drink, let worries flee,
Join in the laughter, feel fancy and free.
Life's a comedy on this sun-kissed shore,
Where smiles are endless, and we're craving more!

Bliss in Every Grain of Sand

Every grain sparkles, they're all in line,
But some are sneaky, they hide like wine.
Flip-flops squeak on the glittery beach,
Making music, a rhythm we can reach.

Sandy toes peek from under the towel,
Tickling the fussers, they just want to growl.
Seashells giggle as we take a pick,
Some shells are shy, while others are slick.

Bikini tops trying their best to stay,
Catch a wave, and they often sway!
The sun's the DJ, spinning the fun,
While laughter echoes, it's a race to run.

Seagulls stealing your chips by the shore,
They squawk in victory while you just roar!
But who could be mad at such a grand show?
Sunshine and giggles, let good vibes flow!

A Quartet of Celestial Rays

Four little suns dance in the sky,
They twirl and twist, and oh, how they fly!
With arms wide open, they reach for the blue,
Tickling the clouds, with laughter anew.

The first one sings with a voice of cheer,
The second tickles, making me veer.
The third brings ice cream, toppings galore,
While the fourth pops up, shining even more.

Together they play, a sibling-like crew,
Splitting the rays, what else can they do?
They splash in the waves, and play peek-a-boo,
Creating shadows, a playful view.

So grab your shades, and dance in delight,
These celestial rays make the days so bright.
In the realm of humor, let's take a bow,
Under their rule, happiness is now!

Footprints of the Horizon

Footprints scatter, like ducks in a row,
Each step a dance, as we go with the flow.
Laughter trails behind, a comical path,
As we chase the tides, escaping their wrath.

A crab in a tux, struts to the beat,
While sandcastles frown, they take a defeat.
With buckets of giggles, we build and we play,
Claiming the beach for an endless array.

The sun laughs above, as we dig and we dive,
Creating our kingdom, where fun is alive!
The horizon smiles with the waves in tow,
Encouraging joy, where good vibes can grow.

As the day fades, the sky turns to gold,
We share silly tales as the night unfolds.
In this breezy haven, we find our way,
Where every footstep invites a new play!

Shores of Endless Warmth

The sun's a big old frying pan,
Flip-flops dance like a wild clan.
Sunscreen debates with my silly hat,
While seagulls plot to steal my snack.

Tanned crabs scuttle with great flair,
Waving claws like they just don't care.
Surfboards wobble and then they crash,
As beach balls soar with a violent splash.

A beach ball's hug is not so grand,
It rolls away to join the sand.
Flip-flop footprints lead the way,
To where my drink had its last say.

The sun sets low in shades of gold,
Tales of fun and laughter told.
Under stars so bright they grin,
Tomorrow comes, let the games begin!

Luminous Shores

The lighthouse winks, it's quite the tease,
I'm tripping over pails and cheese.
A mermaid's laughing by the shore,
With fishy friends, they start to roar.

Sandcastles rise, their turrets tall,
Complaining knights in shell armor call.
Seashells giggle, half-buried deep,
Telling secrets they must keep.

Dolphins leap like jesters' shows,
While jellyfish do silly poses.
The tide pulls back, it's a grand retreat,
But my sandals say they can't be beat.

Crabs perform their sideways dance,
With pinches of joy and a hint of chance.
These lively shores bless all who roam,
In laughter's arms, we find our home!

Whispers of the Eternal Breeze

The breeze whispers jokes that make me grin,
While my hat takes flight, oh where've you been?
Beach balls bounce with a life of their own,
Surf's up, so grab your favorite cone!

My drink's a mix of colors bright,
Like rainbows best before a flight.
But watch those seagulls, they're henchmen bold,
With beaks that sparkle like tales of old.

Flip-flops squeak, a comical tune,
As dolphins dance beneath the moon.
A sandy butt is a badge of charm,
Belly flops bring forth the biggest alarm.

Time ticks slow, yet laughter flies,
As crabby crabs plot funny spies.
With warm thoughts shared in breezy light,
The sun smiles back, enjoying the sight!

Golden Sands and Timeless Waves

Golden sands tickle my toes,
As time drips slowly like honey flows.
Waves crash like laugh tracks, oh so loud,
I'm lost in joy, a very proud crowd.

Sand angels flapping, making their mark,
In this big sandbox, life's pure spark.
Oh, sandcastles with moats filled with pride,
Till sweet little kids send them to the tide.

Buoyant floats do a funky dance,
While curious crabs come take a glance.
The sun's a comedian, brightening the way,
As goofy seagulls steal thoughts of the day.

Under the stars, laughter intertwines,
With good vibes wrapped in coconut lines.
Time here is a joke that never gets old,
In playful warmth, our hearts are bold!

Vistas of Infinite Radiance

In the land where the sun always shines bright,
The seagulls tell jokes that give quite a fright.
Beach balls are bouncing, a colorful sight,
While the crab in a tuxedo dances with might.

Palm trees lean in, they might want a snack,
Whispering secrets while balancing a pack.
The sand's growing warm, in this endless track,
Even the sun says, "Hey, cut me some slack!"

Lemonade rivers flow sweet to the taste,
Sipping too fast? Better slow down with haste.
The fish are in flip-flops, not a moment to waste,
In this sunny haven, no one's ever disgraced.

With laughter and sunshine, the day drifts away,
Time bends and giggles, inviting to play.
In the glow of the moon, we dance and we sway,
Forever on vacation, hip-hip-hooray!

Heartbeat of a Sunlit Paradise

The sun tickles toes, what a silly old game,
Waves crash with laughter, they whisper my name.
A coconut's wearing a hat, how insane!
While the hammock sighs, 'I've got guests, not fame!'

Lizards in shades sip their drinks on the rocks,
They gossip and giggle, all while wearing socks.
Seashells take selfies, perfect frame in a box,
While the frogs throw a party, in green polka dots!

The skies blare a tune, sing along if you dare,
The clouds roll with humor, float high without care.
When the sun sets for fun, life's a colorful fair,
Twinkling with stars, oh what a joke to share!

With umbrellas as hats, we join in the line,
Dancing under lanterns, drink sweet, oh so fine.
Here the laughter flows like the warm sun's shine,
My heart skips a beat, in this paradise divine!

Tales from a Timeless Cove

In a cove where the sun likes to play hide and seek,
The fish wear mustaches, how funny and sleek.
Seashells are storytellers, so curious and cheek,
Each tale makes you chuckle, no need to critique.

The tide rolls in softly, with a giggle or two,
Crabs pass around snacks, a feast just for you.
While the parrot squawks jokes, braving skies so blue,
"Knock, knock!" goes the ocean, guess who's making the cue?

Palm fronds wave their arms, throwing quite a bash,
And sandcastles crumble in a rather funny crash.
The sun winks at twilight, a glorious splash,
As laughter echoes under a sky painted ash.

The zen of the beach, it tickles your soul,
Where moonlit stories begin to unroll.
With friends by your side, let joy take its toll,
In this timeless cove, where we all reach our goal!

A Symphony of Seasonless Love

In this fun-filled world, every moment's a treat,
Where ice cream grows legs and dances on feet.
Friends chase the shadows, how silly, how sweet,
While the sun does a tango, in rhythm, in beat.

Balloons float like dreams, over hot sandy lands,
While flip-flops play tag, with no need for hands.
A chorus of seashells makes quirky demands,
On a stage made of driftwood, where laughter expands.

Rainbows take selfies, there's no hurry to end,
For each wave brings a tune, the tides do commend.
Where sunshine's the DJ, and moments transcend,
In this symphony bright, where fun shall depend.

So come join the dance, let your heart feel the beat,
With laughter like bubbles, our joy is complete.
In a land of endless smiles, playful and neat,
Life flows like a melody, simply so sweet!

Days That Never Fade

On a beach so bright and sunny,
Sandy toes and ice cream, oh so runny.
Seagulls steal fries, what a sight!
Laughing at waves that splash with delight.

Flip-flops squeak as we dance in the sun,
A game of beach ball, oh what fun!
Sun hats flying, out of control,
Chasing shadows, that's our goal!

Each sunset brings a chance to laugh,
With a coconut drink, we take a bath.
Jokes about crabs that walk sideways,
What a life, in these sunny days!

When night falls down, we swap tales grand,
Ghost stories told, as we huddle, hand in hand.
But the ghost turned out, to be a cat,
Oh, the laughter! Just imagine that!

The Rhythm of Eternal Waves

Waves that roll like they own the sea,
Making silly music, set our worries free.
Surfboards wobble, crashing down,
A dolphin giggles, wearing a crown.

Beach umbrellas twirl in the breeze,
Chasing after them is quite the tease.
Tanned folks are running, what a sight!
Gathering their stuff, all in delight.

Flip-flop fashion, who wore it best?
Stripes and polka dots—it's a colorful fest!
A towel fight breaks out, oh dear,
With laughter echoing far and near.

As sun dips low, we break into dance,
Shaking our hips, giving joy a chance.
A flamingo joins in, with a little jig,
Fun never ends; we'll dance real big!

Immortal Skies Above

The sky is painted in pastel hues,
Lucky squirrels sneak a sip, what ruse!
Pineapple hats on heads so bold,
Sipping sweet drinks, chilled and gold.

Clouds float by, wearing silly faces,
Wishing they could join our fun races.
Coconut radios blare a tune,
As we dance beneath a giant moon.

A crab in shades struts on the sand,
Twisting and turning, isn't life grand?
We laugh at the seaweed tangled mess,
Wearing it proudly—oh, what a dress!

The sun says goodbye; it's party time,
Fireflies join in, it's simply sublime.
With each waning glow, we toast our fate,
In these vibrant skies, we celebrate!

Shade of the Timeless Palm

Beneath the palm where shadows play,
Napping iguanas, what do they say?
A hammock swings with effortless grace,
As sunbeams tickle, it's a cozy space.

Lizards don shades, fanciful and bright,
Strutting around like they own the night.
A parrot squawks jokes, oh what a bird!
Leaving listeners in giggles, absurd!

Sipping cool drinks with umbrellas on top,
Feeling the breeze, we never want to stop.
The surging laughter echoes like a song,
In this shade, we simply belong.

As dusk descends with a magical touch,
We share our stories, each silly and such.
With the shadow of the palm, we raise a cheer,
Forever friends, in this vibrant sphere!

The Palette of an Endless Summer

The sun jumped high, what a sight!
With ice cream drips, oh what a fight!
The seagulls squawk, they steal our fries,
While laughter echoes under clear blue skies.

A crab in shorts, what a strange show,
Dancing sideways, putting on a glow.
Flip-flops flying, someone's lost a shoe,
But worry not, there's still a BBQ!

Sunscreen battles, who's the smelly one?
With every splash, we're out for fun.
The waves are giggling, is it just me?
Or did that wave just call out, "Wee!"

Bikini-clad, the dog runs fast,
Chasing after shadows—the good times last.
With each sunset, we'll share a toast,
To the funny moments we love the most.

Eternal Echoes of a Hidden Bay

In a cove where coconuts sway,
We found a treasure—well, kind of cliché.
A bottle of sunblock, half full of sand,
We'll call it gold, isn't it grand?

The pelican misjudged his big dive,
Landed in our cooler, oh how he'd thrive!
With fishy tales that tickle the breeze,
We can't stop laughing, it's a comical tease.

The hammock's swaying, so hard to stay,
The snacks keep calling, come join the fray.
Someone's socks are on the palm tree,
Looks like it's summer with glee, you see?

Beach volleyball? Not our strong suit,
We spike the ball, and we land on loot.
As the sun dips low, laughter rings out,
This hidden bay has fun, without a doubt!

A Celestial Sea of Warm Embrace

The sea is warm like grandma's hug,
With rubber ducks and a giant slug.
Floating umbrellas dance on high,
While seagulls plot a snack heist nearby.

The jellyfish did a funky jig,
While we tried swimming—a funny gig.
Splashes abound, and dives that flop,
We end up laughing, then taking a drop.

A treasure map? Just the beach towel!
Leading to snacks, we yell with a howl.
With every wave, a new surprise,
Like that crab with sunglasses, what a prize!

Sunset arrives with a golden glow,
Painting us silly—what a show!
We raise our drinks, with giggles anew,
In this warm embrace, happiness grew.

Captured by Timeless Rays

Caught in rays that tickle our cheeks,
We chase shadows and play hide-and-seeks.
A sandwich flies, caught in the breeze,
While we can't stop giggling, oh please!

A pufferfish posed for a selfie,
Looking quite spiky but never stealthy.
The sunburned toes look quite bizarre,
As we dance like goofs, under the star.

Lemonade spills, a splash on my head,
My beach hat flies, so I make a bed.
With laughter echoing across the shore,
These timeless rays make us crave more.

As night falls down with a wink and smile,
We'll reminisce here for a while.
Captured by joy, we toast to the day,
Fun is eternal, come what may!

Dance of the Butterflies Under the Sun

In a field where daisies sway,
Butterflies play hide and seek all day.
One lands on a frog's back, oh what a sight!
The frog jumps high, feeling quite light.

They twirl and spin, in colors so bright,
Chasing each other, taking flight.
A caterpillar grumbles, 'I want to join!'
But he's stuck munching leaves, oh what a groin!

The blooms all giggle, they can't help but laugh,
As butterflies dance like they're in a gaff.
With every twist, a surprise they bring,
Even the sun seems to giggle and sing.

An ant on the ground, he's lost in the fun,
Wonders how he's missing the dance in the sun.
But with little legs, he can't keep the pace,
Instead, he just watches, a smile on his face.

The Palette of Infinite Warmth

Colors drip from a funny old bowl,
Sunshine spills like a giggling shoal.
A painter stands scratching his bright, wild head,
Says, 'Where's my blue? Did it run off instead?'

Greens prance around, they dance on the floor,
While oranges roll off, looking to explore.
The sky blushes pink, full of sweet, warm glow,
And says, 'Hey there! I think I'm in a show!'

Yellow jumps up, doing a jig,
While purple just sits, thinking it's big.
The artist just chuckles at colors that blend,
Says, 'You're a riot! We're here for the trend!'

Brushes flick faster, the scene is alive,
With colors so crazy, they manage to thrive.
A canvas full of laughter, a surreal sight,
In this funny dream, they party all night.

Elysian Shores

On golden sands, where laughter shines,
Seagulls giggle, dodging the lines.
A crab in a sunhat waves at a fish,
While octopuses lounge; it's quite the swish!

Children tumble, building castles so grand,
But waves come in fast, as if on command.
The castles collapse with a foamy grin,
And everyone chuckles, let the fun begin!

A palm tree sways, with a drink in its hand,
Sipping coconut juice from the ocean's strand.
While coconuts laugh, falling down with a thud,
It's a beach party complete with soft, warm mud!

Sunset paints jokes across the sky,
As night starts to whisper, a soft lullaby.
Stars pop out, playing hide and peek,
It's a silly night, full of joys unique!

Where the Sun Never Sets

In a land where the sun plays tricks on time,
Chickens wear shades, looking so sublime.
The cows sing ballads, quite off-key,
While pigs breakdance, fancy and free!

The trees are tall with hair made of fluff,
Swaying to music that's silly and tough.
The flowers all giggle with petals so bright,
As the sun winks down, what a magical sight!

A squirrel with sunglasses starts to tap dance,
While rabbits nearby join in for a chance.
They hop and they spin, on this endless day,
Under skies that laugh, come join the display!

Time doesn't rush, it just plays around,
With every tick-tock, a new joke is found.
So come, take a journey where laughter's the key,
In a world where the sun is wild and free!

Secrets Beneath the Mango Trees

Under the trees, where laughter blooms,
Squirrel debates, while the chicken grooms.
The mangoes hide, a sticky delight,
They dare us to climb, in afternoon light.

A parrot squawks and steals my snack,
As I plot a way to get my treat back.
The breeze whispers secrets, so wild and free,
But who'll tell the tales of me in a tree?

Ripe fruits dangle, a sugary tease,
Beneath the shade, we float with ease.
The sun, a jester, plays tricks on the sand,
While we giggle and build, our dreams unplanned.

So here's to the joy, where mischief's a must,
Beneath the mango trees, in laughter we trust.
A paradise found, where every day's sown,
In secrets and giggles, we're never alone.

Radiance of the Unfading Horizon

A sun that shines with a wink and a grin,
Paints the sky orange, where day begins.
Waves on the shore, like clowns in a dance,
Splashing about, they mimic a prance.

Seagulls wear sunglasses, so cool, quite the sight,
While fishing for fries, they're ready to bite.
The horizon chuckles, while sunsets parade,
In hues of bright joy, all worries do fade.

Flip-flops are flying, the game's on the go,
Running in circles, while the soft breezes blow.
With laughter like thunder, we welcome the night,
Fireflies join in, and our hearts take flight.

So raise up your glasses, let's toast to the sun,
In this silly place, we all just have fun.
Forever we'll linger, as stars softly beam,
In a world full of laughter, we'll always redeem.

A Symphony of Sunsets and Stars

As day takes a bow, the colors collide,
The sun spills its secrets, with no need to hide.
Oranges and pinks in a whimsical swirl,
A giggling sky, in a twirling whirl.

Bubbles of laughter float up in the air,
While crickets join in with their evening affair.
The stars pop like popcorn, all shiny and bright,
They've come for a laugh in the cool, gentle night.

Fireworks of joy lit up every face,
A symphony sung with the stars in their place.
With jokes in the wind and dreams on our sleeves,
We dance under twinkling skies, filled with leaves.

So let's make a wish on this magical glow,
Where giggles abound and the silliness flows.
In this concert of bliss, we'll sway to the tune,
Laughing with stars, 'til they sleep with the moon.

The Path of Continuous Joy

Down by the shore, where the giggles echo,
The sand's like a stage for each little show.
We found a sock, and we named it Fred,
Now he's our mascot, with dreams in his head.

Flip-flops applause as we march on the trail,
Following trails where absurdities sail.
With seagulls as guides, we wander and drift,
On this rainbow path, oh, what a gift!

Banana peels tossed, a slip and a slide,
Laughter erupts like a beautiful tide.
Each corner we turn, more silliness found,
With merriment bursting, it knows no bounds.

So join in the fun, let your worries all go,
On this path of giggles, we dance with the flow.
In a world full of joy, let's never be coy,
For life's just a game, and laughter's the toy.

Secrets of the Endless Shore

Flip-flops dancing on the sand,
Seagulls stealing chips from hand.
Sunburns shaped like funny maps,
While crabs crawl in their little naps.

Sandy toes and silly hats,
Ice cream drips on sunburnt pats.
The waves whisper jokes, quite absurd,
To every beachgoer, by a word!

Shells whisper secrets in the breeze,
Tickling noses, making them sneeze.
Beach balls bouncing, laughter so loud,
While dolphins play, drawing a crowd.

At twilight, the sun bows down,
Beach bums laugh, no hint of a frown.
With sandy bites and salty air,
The secrets of fun are everywhere!

Laughter in the Sunlight

Sunshine spills like lemonade,
Beach towels plopped, we've got it made.
Sunglasses worn, but can't see well,
A frisbee lands where folks might yell.

In the ocean, splashes abound,
Kids pretending they're sharks, they hound.
A rubber duck, quite out of place,
Quacking loud, a fowl embrace.

Bikini tops and boardshort mishaps,
Life guards laughing at sun-kissed chaps.
Cranky waves, they take a leap,
Splashing grins while the seagulls peep.

As evening paints the sky with flair,
We tell tall tales with sun-kissed hair.
Pinch me, please, is this a dream?
In laughter's glow, the world's a meme!

Tranquil Tides of the Everlasting

Waves giggle as they kiss the shore,
Turtles race, but no one keeps score.
Seagulls squawk their karaoke tunes,
As sandcastles flirt with shrimpy loons.

Sand in shorts, oh what a sight,
Kites dipped low, a comical flight.
Slathered in sunscreen, we're quite the mess,
But the laughter grows, nonetheless.

Fish frolic with a wink and grin,
We toast to the joy, let the fun begin!
With floats that flip and drinks that spill,
Every hiccup's a thrill and never a chill.

As the twilight chuckles in a blush,
We dance mid-wave, in a silly rush.
With hearts open wide, the day's delights,
In a chorus of giggles, we sail through nights!

Boundless Sunlit Days

Coconuts bob like floating heads,
While tourists nap on their sandy beds.
Sunscreen battles turn quite insane,
As beach balls bounce, causing a rain.

Tommy's wave crashed hard on his face,
His towel now wears a fishy grace.
But laughter erupts like a bubble bath,
In the sun's warm, inviting path.

Picnic ants in a tiny parade,
Join the party, there's joy to be made.
Watermelons roll and seeds take flight,
As everyone giggles, clueless of fright.

As stars appear in a cosmic dance,
We share stories that make us prance.
With sun-drenched smiles and hearts so light,
These days of fun glitter in the night!

Gentle Waves of Timelessness

The sun tickles toes in the golden sand,
While seagulls perform their silly dance.
Flip-flops fly as kids take a stand,
Waves crash in laughter, they seize the chance.

Beach balls bounce and sunscreen flies,
Chasing crabs with goofy grins.
The tide laughs back, it never sighs,
In this timeless game, everyone wins.

Shells are hats, and shovels a sword,
As pirates plot for treasure unknown.
The ocean's laughter, a sweet reward,
Where worries retreat and joy has grown.

So let's sip coconuts, feel the breeze,
Trade giggles for fish and sunburned skin.
In this universe of giggly ease,
Each moment's a party—we all dive in!

Moments that Melt like Ice Cream

Under the sun, the ice cream drips,
On cone hats, laughter's the flavor today.
Sticky fingers and sweet little lips,
As giggles parade and dreams come out to play.

Chocolate rivers and vanilla lakes,
Swirl of flavors in every splash.
Neighborhood kids making silly stakes,
Who can juggle the most before a crash?

Melted puddles reflect our cheer,
As sprinkles scatter like stars that fell.
Here on the couch, all worries disappear,
In an ice cream dream, we laugh and dwell.

So grab a scoop, let the fun begin,
Children of summer, carefree and bold.
We'll create a world where we all win,
In moments that melt and never grow old.

The Magic of Unbroken Days

A beach ball bounds in the splendid air,
While flip-flops squeak in a quirky song.
Time does a jig without a care,
As laughter twirls and the day feels long.

Sunbeams skip like kids on a spree,
Painting the sky with giggles and light.
While jellyfish bob like they're free,
Every hour's a treat, wrapped up just right.

Sunkissed picnics with fruits in a row,
Sandcastles rise to rival the sun.
Lobster hats and clam shells aglow,
In a land of play, we've all just begun.

So gather your dreams like seashells bright,
In this kingdom where fun's on display.
Magic extends in the soft twilight,
In the magic of days that never decay!

Cherished Dreams in the Comfort of Light

Twinkling lights on the water's embrace,
As laughter ripples like waves in the night.
Pineapple boats race, a silly chase,
Where dreams are afloat in shimmering sight.

Worms in wigs join the dance of glee,
With coconut drums beating time by the sea.
Ghost crabs with sass have a nightcap spree,
While the moon wears shades, as cool as can be.

Palms sway to the giggling breeze,
Whispering secrets with each little sway.
In cozy corners, hearts feel at ease,
As cherished dreams lead us ever astray.

So let's catch the stars and spin them around,
In an evening of whimsy, let's take flight.
With the comfort of laughter, joy knows no bound,
In this paradise, everything feels right!

The Sunflower Pathway

Bumblebees waltz in a golden spree,
Sunflowers giggle at my clumsy glee.
Flip-flops flop on my dancing feet,
While ants play tag, oh what a treat!

Lemonade stands offering a sweet embrace,
I spill my drink all over the place.
But who needs a cup when the sun's so hot?
A sticky situation? Not a big plot!

Each corn dog twist is a bombastic whirl,
Cotton candy clouds make my head twirl.
I chase the seagulls, they wave and flee,
"Catch me if you can!" they laugh with glee!

As the sun dips low, I trip and slide,
In a puddle of laughter, I take great pride.
A sunset glow paints the sky with cheer,
On this whimsy path, there's nothing to fear!

Vibrant Hues of Forever

Crayon skies and a paintbrush sea,
A rainbow of laughs, come splash with me!
Marshmallow clouds float overhead,
While jellybean breezes tickle my head.

The sun wears shades like a cool cat,
As goofballs hop in their beach ball hats.
Seashells whisper jokes as they roll,
Each wave a chuckle, a tickling soul.

Ice cream cones turn into sticky goo,
Melting away, oh what to do?
A squirrel snaps selfies, a digital pro,
While I chase the ice cream truck down below!

The vibrant hues spin a silly tale,
Of flip-flops flying and boat rides frail.
With every twist of this silly quest,
Life's kaleidoscope keeps us blessed!

Seasons of Unceasing Delight

Flip-flops click on a sun-kissed street,
Grass stains and giggles, oh what a feat!
The ice cream truck plays a joyful tune,
While we chase it down like a cartoon.

Sandy toes and a frisbee fight,
"Catch that wave!" I shout in pure delight.
But the seagulls swoop in, what a sight!
Stealing our snacks, they take flight!

Hats fly high like balloons in June,
While we dance to the ocean's swoon.
Kites in the air perform a ballet,
Against the backdrop of a shining day.

Laughter echoes as the sunset glows,
We share silly stories, anything goes!
In this land of laughter and glee,
Each moment is magic, wild and free!

Chronicles of Sandy Bliss

Once upon a time on a sandy shore,
I built a castle, but alas, it bore!
A wave came crashing, oh what a mess,
Now it's a moat—a sandy caress!

With a boogie board, I try to glide,
But end up tumbling—a silly ride.
Starfish giggle as they watch my plight,
While crabs applaud in their sideways flight.

Sunsets drip like honey, slow and sweet,
My friends and I play pictionary on our feet.
"Draw a unicorn!" someone shouts with flair,
But I make a toaster—it's quite rare!

As night falls, we roast marshmallows bright,
Telling tall tales underneath starry light.
Laughter and warmth, a fantastic blend,
In these chronicles, the fun won't end!

The Horizon's Endless Glow

The sun's so bright it wears a frown,
It never sets; just bounces 'round.
Flip-flops flop as seagulls squawk,
Dancing shadows on the dock.

Palm trees wave like they've gone mad,
While beach balls bounce, it's all quite rad.
Sandy toes and sunscreen dreams,
Life here's bursting at the seams.

Every wave's a joke on shore,
Each splash a laugh, who could want more?
Laughter rises with the tide,
Sun-rays glow, like joy we bide.

With ice cream dripping down my hand,
I chase the clouds that look like sand.
In this warm, perpetual bliss,
I've lost my hat, but gained a kiss.

Serene Sanctuary Beneath Golden Skies

Beneath a sun that's ripe and round,
The tourists tumble, trip, and bound.
A piña colada in each hand,
Life's too short to make a plan!

The beach towels spread like jelly beans,
And everyone's drinking from big machines.
A little sunburn's just a thrill,
Who cares? We've got time to kill!

The seagulls gossip, strut, and preen,
While sunbathers bask in shades of green.
With laughter echoing in the breeze,
I swap my towel for a tease!

As sunset's hues start to appear,
I toast a coconut, let out a cheer.
In the glow of this silken light,
Who knew paradise could be so bright?

A Tapestry of Warmth

The heat's a prankster, oh so sly,
Chasing away clouds in the sky.
Tickled toes in warm, soft sand,
I grab a drink; it's all unplanned!

Bikinis and board shorts dance in tune,
While surfboards float like a shy balloon.
A beach ball flies but lands with a smack,
Lost my lunch? No, just a snack!

Sunscreen battles then ensue,
As beach umbrellas hide from the view.
Bright flip-flops hop, and giggles sprout,
In a circus of fun, there's never doubt.

With laughter spilling like warm waves,
The silly whales peek out of caves.
Sizzle and serve; let the funny rise,
Life's too short—eat cake and fries!

Radiant Haven

In a place where the sun's too loud,
And laughter swells, a boisterous crowd.
Sunglasses perched on noses bright,
We dance away the day and night.

Margaritas won the party prize,
As the pineapple jokes arise.
Shells gossip about the stars' flair,
While flip-flops shiver without a care.

The sun's a joker in the sky,
It tickles clouds as they drift by.
With sandy castles and mermaids glee,
We'll laugh until the last cup's free.

As day ends with a playful wink,
We raise our cups, let our spirits sink.
In this radiant cove, how sweet,
The fun, my friend, is quite the treat!

www.ingramcontent.com/pod-product-compliance
Lightning Source LLC
Chambersburg PA
CBHW072220070526
44585CB00015B/1414